W9-ARH-276

ESSENTIAL LIBRARY OF
AMERICAN
WARS

WORLD WAR I

ABDO
Publishing Company

WORLD WAR I

BY MARY K. PRATT

CONTENT CONSULTANT

Steven Sabol
Associate Professor of History, UNC Charlotte

CREDITS

Published by ABDO Publishing Company, PO Box 398166, Minneapolis, MN 55439. Copyright © 2014 by Abdo Consulting Group, Inc. International copyrights reserved in all countries. No part of this book may be reproduced in any form without written permission from the publisher. The Essential Library™ is a trademark and logo of ABDO Publishing Company.

Printed in the United States of America,
North Mankato, Minnesota
052013
092013

 THIS BOOK CONTAINS AT LEAST 10% RECYCLED MATERIALS.

Editor: Arnold Ringstad
Series Designer: Emily Love

Photo Credits

AP Images, cover, 2, 6, 27, 33, 38, 46, 54, 80, 84, 98 (right); Fotosearch/Getty Images, 10, 99 (right); US Marine Corps, 14; Library of Congress, 16, 41; C. Turner Beckett, 19; Bettmann/Corbis/AP Images, 21, 25, 53, 56, 66, 70, 87, 90, 96, 98 (left), 99 (left); Harris & Ewing/Library of Congress, 28, 101 (left); Topical Press Agency/Hulton Archive/Getty Images, 44; National Archives, 60, 64; US Army Signal Corps/Time Life Pictures/Getty Images, 75; Paul Popper/Popperfoto/Getty Images, 77; US Army, 79; Leonard Raven-Hill, 94; Red Line Editorial, 100, 101 (top); Imperial War Museum, 101 (right)

Library of Congress Control Number: 2013932677

Cataloging-in-Publication Data

Pratt, Mary K.
 World War I / Mary K. Pratt.
   p. cm. -- (Essential library of American wars)
Includes bibliographical references and index.
ISBN 978-1-61783-881-1
1. World War, 1914-1918--History--Juvenile literature. World War, 1914-1918--Europe--Juvenile literature. I. Title.
940.3--dc23

                                                    2013932677

CONTENTS

TRIAL BY FIRE

It was May 30, 1918. Nearly four brutal years into World War I, the Allied British and French troops were entrenched in a war against Germany. Each side hoped for decisive battles that would force the other side to surrender or at least negotiate for peace. By late May, it appeared the Germans were poised to win.

The Allied troops became demoralized as the Germans claimed several military victories that spring. The United States had joined the Allies in 1917, but it seemed to be making little difference so far. The Germans had captured the French village of Seicheprey from the Americans, and they had pushed the weakened French troops back more than 30 miles (48 km).[1] More than 1 million civilians fled Paris on the first two days of June, fearful the Germans would soon invade France's capital city.[2]

By 1918, World War I had left a wide swath of Europe in ruins.

John Pershing was born in Laclede, Missouri, on September 13, 1860. He attended the US Military Academy at West Point, graduating in 1882. Pershing served in the US wars against American Indians on the Great Plains from 1886 to 1891, and then served in Cuba during the Spanish-American War (1898). President Theodore Roosevelt promoted him to the rank of brigadier general in 1906. In that position, he commanded US troops in the Philippines and Mexico. In Mexico, Pershing led cavalry forces pursuing the Mexican revolutionary general known as Pancho Villa after Villa launched an attack on Americans inside the United States in 1916.

President Woodrow Wilson named Pershing commander of the American Expeditionary Forces—the American armies sent to Europe during World War I—in 1917. After the war, Pershing was promoted to general of the armies, the highest possible rank in the army. Pershing retired in 1924 and died on July 15, 1948, having lived from before the American Civil War (1861–1865) until after World War II (1939–1945).

US Army general John Pershing received an urgent request from French general Philippe Pétain. Pétain needed US troops to help stop the German advance that had broken through the French lines. The German forces were nearing Paris and fighting fiercely in the hopes they could capture the city and force the French to surrender. The French forces were fighting fiercely, too. But they were tired and their numbers were depleted. Approximately 60,000 French soldiers had been captured in recent battles.[3] France was looking at a possible defeat after four long years of war against Germany and the other Central powers. It was counting on the United States to keep it from losing the war.

INTO THE FRAY

The US troops immediately took action. Pershing ordered two American divisions to move to the battlefield, an area near the Marne River approximately 50 miles (80 km) northwest of Paris. The troops arrived early on June 1 only to find hundreds of French refugees trying to escape the Germans. The fleeing civilians warned the Americans about the dangers they would face, telling them they were marching to their deaths. But the Americans were undeterred. Marine Captain Lloyd Williams remarked: "Retreat, hell. We just got here."[4] The American troops moved forward, assembling near the village of Vaux and a small forest called Belleau Wood. Here, in the 200-acre (80 ha) forest, US soldiers would encounter some of the fiercest, bloodiest fighting of the war.[5]

Brushing aside demands from France to have US troops fight under French command, Pershing committed his own forces to the battle. One of his divisions took up positions along a ten-mile (16 km) stretch of the Marne River.[6] Meanwhile, the other division, which included a brigade of US Marines, moved

toward Belleau Wood under the command of Major General Omar Bundy.

French troops continued fighting the German forces for several more days. On June 4, 1918, French leaders withdrew the exhausted French troops from the front lines and turned the area over to one of the American divisions. Bundy planned to lead an attack on the Germans to capture a ridge on the western edge of Belleau Wood called Hill 142. Afterward, he would take Belleau Wood itself.

American troops, led by US Marines, attacked

MARINES ON THE FRONT LINES

The Marine Corps had traditionally served as a fighting force aboard naval ships, but by 1917 the Corps had an image as the "First to Fight," as its unofficial motto says. This reputation as an elite fighting force helped the Marines recruit men during World War I. In fact, 239,274 men applied to join the Marines during the war; the Marines accepted only 60,189 of them.[7] However, General Pershing assigned the first Marines who arrived in France to jobs working security posts and dock jobs, such as unloading ships and trucks. But the Marines soon joined the fighting on the front lines. They quickly distinguished themselves as fierce combatants, and in the Battle of Belleau Wood they gained a new reputation as America's elite troops, living up to their "First to Fight" motto.[8]

A marine takes aim during the Battle of Belleau Wood.

Reporters were among the first to declare the Battle of Belleau Wood a victory for the United States. On June 6, the *Chicago Daily Tribune* declared: "U.S. Marines Smash Huns," Huns being a derogatory name for the Germans. The *New York Times* proclaimed the next day: "Our Marines Attack, Gain Mile at Veuilly."[9] The reporting highlighted the role of the Marines at the battle. Army leadership prohibited reporters from identifying army divisions and units. The army said journalists could not report anything about the number of troops in their stories, either. But journalists noted that the Marines were not part of the army, even though they made up a sizable portion of one of the US divisions. Since the Marines did not share the army's restrictions on reporting, journalists were able to learn more about Marine involvement in the battle. As a result, much of the news coverage about the Battle of Belleau Wood highlighted the Marines' successes without as much mention of the army's contributions.

the Germans on Hill 142 in the early morning hours of June 6. Americans also attacked the Germans at the nearby village of Bouresches, on the eastern edge of Belleau Wood. US military leaders made several mistakes as the battle started. First, they underestimated the number of Germans in the area. They also ordered the attack before they had all of their troops and machine guns in place, and they instructed the men to march in waves straight into the German machine-gun fire. Despite these errors and old-fashioned tactics, the Marines were able to take Hill 142 by midday.

They spent the rest of the day defending the hill from German counterattacks.

Although the Marines successfully took Hill 142, the victory had not come easily. They suffered a total of 1,087 men killed or wounded.[10] At the time, it was the highest casualty count in a single day in Marine Corps history. June 6, 1918, remained the Marines' bloodiest day for 25 years, until they suffered even higher losses during World War II.[11]

The battle for Hill 142 was only the beginning. The fight for Belleau Wood itself would last for another 19 days, with US troops fighting through heavily forested terrain, with dense undergrowth and boulders blocking movement and vision. The Americans had little water and no hot food, and the constant stench of decaying bodies hung in the air. The Germans fought ferociously, attacking the Americans with artillery, machine guns, and poison gas. When the two sides got close enough, the Marines found themselves in hand-to-hand combat with the Germans using bayonets and knives. The Marines finally took Belleau Wood from the Germans on June 25. A battalion commander reported the next day: "Woods now U.S. Marine Corps entirely."[12]

HONORING THE MARINES OF BELLEAU WOOD

In recognition of their victory at Belleau Wood, the French awarded the American forces unit citations for "gallant action."[13] The French also officially changed the name of the forest from Belleau Wood to Bois de la Brigade Marine, or Wood of the Marine Brigade. In July 1923, the area was dedicated as an American battle monument.

The American victory at Belleau Wood did not bring about the immediate end of World War I. But it did halt the German march toward Paris and save France from possible defeat. Still, peace between the Allies and the Central powers would cost the lives of thousands more Marines and US soldiers.

Marines rest after achieving victory at Belleau Wood.

A SHOOTING
IN SARAJEVO

When the 1900s dawned, the new century seemed to promise an era of prosperity and international trade. Factories in Europe and the United States were making and selling new manufactured goods, such as cars. South Africa exported gold and diamonds, Australia sold wool from sheep, and Malaysia harvested rubber. New and better modes of transportation carried these products around the globe. Steamships, traveling faster than sailing ships, became the most common way to cross oceans. Their speed meant more goods could be transported to more countries more quickly. And the railroads built in the late 1800s meant products could travel to people living in many landlocked parts of the Americas, Europe, and Asia. Even people moved around more. Twenty-six million people emigrated from Europe to

International exhibitions, such as the one held in Paris in 1900, allowed nations to showcase their technical advances and demonstrated their optimism for the new century.

the Americas and Australia between 1890 and 1910.[1] And more people began traveling to other countries to see historic and cultural sights. Business and political leaders believed increased cooperation between nations would make countries better, richer, and more peaceful.

However, this optimism ran counter to the European wars fought in the decades leading up to World War I. In the Franco-Prussian War (1870–1871), Germany fought and defeated France. After the war, Germany took from France a province called Alsace and part of a province called Lorraine.

More fighting took place in the Balkans in 1912 and 1913, an area in southeastern Europe that included the countries of Serbia, Bulgaria, and Romania. The Balkans had fought and won their independence from Turkey and the Ottoman Empire. But subsequently, the Austro-Hungarian Empire took control of parts of the Balkans. The seizure upset Russia, because Russia also wanted to control the Balkans.

AMERICAN CONFLICTS

Conflict was not limited to Europe; the United States had its share of fighting with other countries in the decades prior to World War I. In the spring of 1898, the US Congress declared

American soldiers march home following the Pancho Villa expedition into Mexico.

war on Spain, largely over the Caribbean nation of Cuba. The United States backed the Cubans who wanted Spain out of their island nation, which lay just off the American coast near Florida. Fighting occurred in both Cuba and the Philippines. The war was brief, and Spain surrendered in August 1898.

The United States also had military skirmishes with Mexico and Mexican rebels in the early 1900s. In one incident, Pancho Villa led hundreds of Mexican soldiers in an attack on US soldiers and civilians in Columbus, New Mexico, on March 9, 1916. President Woodrow Wilson ordered Brigadier General Pershing to Mexico to help capture Villa. Pershing was unable to capture Villa, and the United States and Mexico remained on unfriendly terms because of the incident.

THE WAR BEGINS

These disputes between countries increased tensions around the world, creating the conditions that allowed a relatively minor incident to ignite World War I. On June 28, 1914, an assassin shot and killed Archduke Franz Ferdinand, heir to the Austro-Hungarian Empire. Ferdinand was in Sarajevo, a city in the province of Bosnia. Part of the Balkans, Bosnia was then ruled by Austria-Hungary. Ferdinand and his wife, Sophie, were riding in a car along a street lined by people when someone threw a small bomb at their procession of cars. The bomb exploded and injured several people, but it failed to hurt Ferdinand. Later that day, he traveled to the hospital to visit the injured. It was then that 19-year-old Gavrilo Princip shot and killed Ferdinand and his wife.

Princip was one of six young men who had planned to assassinate Ferdinand that day. The six were born and grew up in Bosnia, but they were of Serbian descent. They belonged to a group called Young Bosnia that wanted independence for the Serbs in the Balkans. Investigators determined the young men

Police arrested Gavrilo Princip after he assassinated Archduke Franz Ferdinand.

obtained their weapons in Serbia, a small country bordering Bosnia. Historians have not been able to determine whether the Serbian government knew about the plot to kill Ferdinand, but Austro-Hungarian leaders decided they had to punish Serbia for the assassination.

If Austria-Hungary had taken immediate action against Serbia, the assassination of Ferdinand might have become a little-known historical incident of no real significance. But instead, the two countries drew other nations into their dispute. Austro-Hungarian leaders asked Germany to support a war against Serbia. Russia, which shared a Slavic ethnicity with the Serbians, decided to defend Serbia. France had a treaty with Russia that said it would side with Russia in a war against Germany. The United Kingdom had a treaty that said it would help France. And Germany, Austria-Hungary, and Italy had a treaty that said they would all fight if any of them went to war against two other nations.

Austria-Hungary declared war on Serbia on July 28, 1914. Soon other countries entered the war, too. The United Kingdom, France, and Russia became known as the Allies. Austria-Hungary and Germany were called the Central powers. The news of war came as a surprise to most of the average citizens in those countries. Few could have imagined the extent of the death and devastation the war declarations would bring to the world.

EARLY BATTLES

Fighting quickly erupted in Europe. On August 2, 1914, German cavalry invaded the small country of Luxembourg and seized its railroads. That same day, Germany informed Belgium that it wanted to march its armies through the small country. King Albert of Belgium refused, ordering his army to blow up bridges and rail lines to slow the advancing German armies. However, the Germans had two new weapons: the 305-mm Skoda siege mortar and the 420-mm howitzer, nicknamed "Big Bertha." These massive cannons had never been used in battle before, but the German forces soon used them against the Belgian troops and fortifications, displaying just how powerfully destructive they were.

While Germany was attacking Luxembourg and Belgium, France was preparing troops for battle on the front lines of what became known as the Western Front. France placed more than 1 million

THE CHRISTMAS TRUCE

The horrors of war came to a brief halt at Christmastime in 1914 as Belgian, British, French, and German soldiers on the front lines observed the holiday. The first holiday observances happened near the Belgian city of Ypres. German soldiers sang Christmas carols and displayed bits of decorated evergreens. British troops reported seeing strange lights near the German trenches and thought the Germans were preparing to attack. But the British soon realized the Germans were putting up Christmas trees decorated with candles. The British and French troops started singing Christmas carols, too. Both sides used the unofficial truce to gather and bury the dead. At one funeral held along the front lines, Allied and German soldiers prayed together. Commanding officers did not share the holiday spirit, however. They ordered an end to the practice and threatened punishments if it ever happened again.

troops along its border with the German provinces of Alsace and Lorraine.[2] The United Kingdom declared war on Germany on August 2, 1914. It drew soldiers from all over its empire, including Australia, India, and Canada, and sent them to fight in France. Austria-Hungary invaded Serbia, which launched counterattacks against the invading troops. And Russia moved its troops into Prussia, on the eastern side of Germany. This area, where combat between German and Russian troops took place, was the Eastern Front.

The fighting along the Eastern and Western fronts proved equally bloody. Heavy artillery and rapid-fire machine guns led to a

POISON GAS

At 5:00 p.m. on April 22, 1915, African troops fighting in the French trenches saw a grey-green cloud drifting across no-man's-land toward them. Soon, thousands of the soldiers were coughing and gasping for breath. They abandoned their posts, leaving an 8,000-yard (7,300 m) gap in the French front lines.[3] The attack marked the first use of lethal poison gas. The French soon identified the gas as chlorine. The Allies followed with their own use of poison gas. Both the Allies and the Germans used phosgene and mustard gases during the war, and by 1918 roughly one in every four shells fired on the Western Front contained poison gas.[4] The gas shells could kill soldiers and blister their skin, but soldiers on both sides began using alarms and gas masks to prepare themselves for the attacks.

After the introduction of poison gas to the war, gas masks became essential equipment for soldiers on the front lines.

staggering number of casualties, outpacing the expectations of military leaders.

Commanders also failed to anticipate the stalemate that emerged. Troops dug into dirt trenches rimmed with barbed wire, leaving a space known as no-man's-land between the warring sides. They bombarded each other with shells and, later in the war, poison gas. They launched attacks and counterattacks, often winning and losing the same small strip of ground over the course of multiple battles. The war continued to rage, but no nation was able to win a big enough victory on the battlefield to force the other countries to surrender.

More countries joined the war. Italy joined the Allies in May 1915, agreeing to fight after Allied leaders promised Italy territory from Austria-Hungary following victory. Greece and Romania joined the Allies in 1916.

A GLOBAL WAR

World War I drew in countries beyond Europe, too. Turkey entered the war on November 3, 1914, on the side of the Central powers. Turkish soldiers fought Russian troops in southern Russia and other Allied forces in the Middle East. Turkey killed some of its own people, too, starting on April 25, 1915. Turkish authorities saw the Armenians living in the nation's northeast region as enemies and over the next two years forced them from their homes and into the Mesopotamian deserts. The Turks massacred thousands of Armenian men, women, and children. Historians estimate more than 1 million Armenians were killed between 1916 and 1923.[5]

Fighting over the European nations' colonies brought the war to nearly all corners of the world. At the time, European countries had colonized most of Africa. British and French forces, including Africans drafted into the war, attacked and overran Germany's four African colonies. In the Far East,

By 1916, Europe's major powers had chosen
sides or decided to remain neutral.

Japan entered the war on the side of the Allies. Seeking greater
influence, the recently modernized Japanese military seized
German colonies in the Pacific and attacked German ships.

THE UNITED STATES ENTERS THE CARNAGE

War engulfed Europe during the late summer of 1914, but the United States managed to remain neutral. Many Americans advocated not just for neutrality but for the country to remain isolationist, or completely separate economically and politically from the other nations of the world. Some Americans, including Secretary of State William Jennings Bryan, were pacifists. They opposed war and violence in every case because of ethical, moral, or religious convictions. President Wilson himself campaigned for reelection in 1916 on a platform advocating for peace. One of his campaign slogans was "Not one American boy to the

President Woodrow Wilson reviews US Army troops. Wilson initially pledged to keep the United States out of war, but volatile world events would lead to a change in policy.

European war."[1] Other Americans, though, were sympathetic to one side or the other. Some sided more with the Allies. They faulted Germany for invading Belgium and killing civilians, while some sided with France as a result of France's past support of the United States. Others were not as sympathetic to the Allies, harboring a distrust of the United Kingdom that dated back to the American Revolution (1775–1783). They saw Britain's naval blockade of Germany and neutral European countries as an aggressive act.

Despite conflicting opinions among Americans, the United States remained out of the war into the conflict's third year. But the United States was not

PRESIDENT WOODROW WILSON

Woodrow Wilson was born in Virginia in 1856. He was the son of a Presbyterian minister who had served as a pastor in Augusta, Georgia, during the Civil War. Wilson's father supported the Confederacy and owned slaves. Wilson attended Princeton University and then the University of Virginia Law School and Johns Hopkins University. In 1902, he became the president of Princeton.

He ran for president in 1912, stressing individualism and the rights of states to avoid interference from the federal government. He won reelection in 1916 by campaigning with the slogan "he kept us out of war."[2] Soon after reelection, though, he sought Congress's declaration of war against Germany. Wilson, who served as president throughout World War I, died in 1924.

fully isolated. It had been expanding its national reach overseas for several decades, engaging in overseas military and political actions. It had fought over Cuba in the Spanish-American War in 1898. And it had joined other countries in using military force to quell the Chinese protesters who were fighting against foreign influence in their country. Americans were also engaged in commercial trade with Allied countries during the first years of World War I. American companies sold goods used in military operations, including ammunition and guns, to the United Kingdom and France.

A NEW AMERICAN ARMY

As US politicians and military leaders debated the country's preparedness for a potential war in Europe, the US Congress passed what was then the most comprehensive military legislation in American history: the National Defense Act of 1916.

The law, which provided for a larger army during times of both peace and war, allowed for a fourfold expansion of the National Guard. In addition, the law authorized the president to mobilize the National Guard during times of war or national emergency. It also authorized the peacetime army to increase in size to 175,000 men over five years, with a wartime size of nearly 300,000.[3] This increased size was still dwarfed by the sizes of the armies in the European countries already engaged in World War I.

PREPARING FOR WAR

But the United States would not stay out of the carnage forever. From the early part of the war, its leaders began preparing for what seemed like the country's inevitable entrance into the war. The earlier international actions of the United States, including the country's expanding interests in the Pacific Ocean, had resulted in a modernized army and navy by the time World War I began. By 1917, the US Navy was the third largest in the world, just behind the British and German navies.[4] In the early 1900s, the US Army began equipping its units with rapid-firing machine guns; in 1916, Congress approved spending $12 million on machine guns.[5]

Still, for the first few years of World War I the fighting remained thousands of miles away from the shores of the United States. But Americans were increasingly becoming involved. On May 7, 1915, a German submarine torpedoed a British steamship, the *Lusitania*. Some 1,198 people, including 128 Americans, were killed when the ship sank.[6]

Following the sinking of the *Lusitania*, many Americans who had been neutral began supporting the notion of going to war. Americans were already aware of how much destruction had been caused by the fighting. The warring nations had started

The *Lusitania* was only a few miles from the shore of Ireland when it was sunk.

using poison gas against each other, causing painful deaths and horrific injuries. Some battles were inflicting casualties in such high numbers the countries tallied the number of dead and

STORIES FROM THE WAR

Walter Schwieger, the commander of the submarine that sank the *Lusitania*, kept a diary onboard his ship. Here, he describes the *Lusitania* sinking:

"Clear bow shot at 700 [meters]. . . . Shot struck starboard side close behind the bridge. An extraordinarily heavy detonation followed, with a very large cloud of smoke (far above the front funnel). A second explosion must have followed that of the torpedo (boiler or coal or powder?). . . . The ship stopped immediately and quickly listed sharply to starboard, sinking deeper by the head at the same time. It appeared as if it would capsize in a short time. Great confusion arose on the ship; some of the boats were swung clear and lowered into the water."[7]

wounded in the hundreds of thousands.[8] Yet the countries of Europe were locked in a stalemate, attaining some victories and suffering some defeats but never achieving the kind of definitive wins on the battlefield that would finally end the war.

STAYING NEUTRAL

Germany, desperate because of the continued blockade of its ports by the British, decided in early 1917 to resume torpedoing any ships it found in the waters off the British Isles and France. On January 31, 1917, Germany told US leaders its submarines would sink all vessels they found without warning. At least one German military leader spoke against such unrestricted torpedoing

GERMAN WARNINGS

Even though Americans were angered by the sinking of the *Lusitania*, the German attack was hardly a surprise. Germany had warned the United States it would take such action. First, on February 4, Germany declared it considered the waters around the British Isles a war zone. On April 22, the German Embassy in the United States published warnings in US newspapers saying those traveling on Allied ships were doing so at their own risk. After the sinking of the *Lusitania*, Germany agreed to only torpedo passenger liners after warning them and promising they would have safeguards for passengers' lives. But Germany resumed its policy of torpedoing ships without restrictions by early 1917.

because he feared it would bring the United States into the war against Germany. Other German commanders saw the unrestricted sinking of ships as a way to finally defeat the Allies.

US leaders, including President Wilson, continued to keep the United States out of the war even as Germany launched its campaign of unrestricted submarine warfare in the Atlantic. Then came news of a message British officials had intercepted. The message was the Zimmerman telegram, sent from Germany to Mexico and named for Germany's foreign secretary. Germany proposed that if the United States entered the war, Mexico should enter the war on the side of Germany. In return, Germany would offer Mexico financial support. If the German-Mexican alliance won the war, the telegram said, Mexico would be allowed to retake Texas, New Mexico, and Arizona from the United States. The news of this message was revealed in February 1917, enraging many Americans. Still, the United States stayed out of the war.

JOINING THE ALLIES

Teetering on the edge, the United States finally had enough when German submarines sank four American ships in early spring 1917. President Wilson, who had promoted a platform of peace, called together his advisers. They spoke in favor of war.

On April 2, 1917, Wilson delivered a speech to Congress, saying war was unavoidable. Four days later, on April 6, the United States declared war on Germany. But as the country readied its troops, many in Europe wondered whether the United States could end the gruesome slaughter and bring an end to the bloody stalemate.

PRESIDENT WILSON ADDRESSES CONGRESS

For the first three years of World War I, President Wilson worked to keep the United States out of the war. But by spring 1917, the president felt that policy was no longer appropriate. He explained his position in an April 2 address to Congress:

> Neutrality is no longer feasible or desirable where the peace of the world is involved and the freedom of its peoples, and the menace to that peace and freedom lies in the existence of autocratic governments backed by organized force which is controlled wholly by their will, not by the will of their people. We have seen the last of neutrality in such circumstances.[9]

THE UNITED STATES AT WAR

At the outbreak of World War I, the United States was unprepared for war. It had a small army, with 130,000 men in the regular army and 70,000 in the National Guard.[1] To ready the nation for war, Congress passed the Selective Service Act on May 19, 1917. The act required men between the ages of 18 and 45 to register with the government for possible drafting into the military. More than 24 million men registered, and 2.8 million of them served in the military during American involvement in World War I.[2] More than half were volunteers.[3] Some men joined the military because they saw it as a chance for adventure or wanted to right the wrongs happening in Europe. Others volunteered because they felt pressured by family, friends, and community members who believed it was their duty to join the military and fight in the war.

Following the declaration of war, the US government immediately put into motion its plans to draft the millions of men it would need to fight in Europe.

THE UNITED STATES FINANCES THE WAR

World War I had a financial impact on the United States in more ways than one when the nation declared war on Germany in 1917. In addition to the US government having to pay for its own troops and supplies, the US Congress passed a law that allowed the country to loan the other Allied countries money to help them pay for their war efforts. Congress passed the first Loan Act on April 24, 1917. It authorized the United States to add $5 billion to its own debt to pay for the war-related bills of the United States and its allies. Congress passed 30 more laws like it before the war ended.[5]

Some Americans had been fighting in World War I long before the United States officially joined the battle. A few joined the British and Canadian armies, while others enlisted in the French Foreign Legion. A group of American pilots formed a group called the Lafayette Escadrille and became part of the French air force. Germans protested against individual Americans joining the Allied ranks, saying it was against the US government's official position of neutrality. But Germany's protests did not keep out such American volunteers.

All told, an estimated 25,000 Americans fought in France on the side of the British and French before the United States entered World War I.[4]

Georges Thenault, *second from left*, was the French commander of the mostly American Lafayette Escadrille.

UNPREPARED FOR BATTLE

Many did not expect the United States to send a large number of men from its army to Europe to fight. Even after the country declared war on Germany, the Allies thought the United States would be most helpful by lending them more money and equipment—something the United States had been doing throughout the war. In fact, some British and French military officers thought they could still win the war without the United States contributing a large military force. For its part, the United States did not have plans in place to send a lot of troops to Europe. Its military plans focused mostly on defending the United States.

But the situation changed quickly after the United States entered the war. The United Kingdom and France asked for American soldiers to fight alongside their own forces under British and French command. American military leaders refused to give other countries such control over American forces. Instead, the United States built up its military and sent more than 2 million men to France.[6] They made up the American Expeditionary Forces (AEF).

Getting the men ready for the task was not easy. As the country entered the war, the military did not have enough rifles to arm its new soldiers. Some soldiers had to train with wooden guns. The country did not have enough artillery shells, either. The United States' entire stockpile of artillery shells would have been used up in just nine hours of battle.[7] The United States also lacked the cannons needed to launch the shells, and it could not get American foundries to make more artillery pieces fast enough. The United States ended up buying guns and artillery from the British and French.

American troops seemed unprepared even when they arrived in France. Their uniforms did not fit properly. They did not show the same military precision the British, French, and German troops displayed when marching and parading. They did not have basic equipment, such as winter clothes or gas masks to help them survive poison gas attacks. There were also delays and bottlenecks getting men and equipment off the ships. The first US troops, nicknamed "doughboys," arrived at Saint Nazaire, France, on June 28, 1917.

INTO THE STALEMATE

The US troops landed in the middle of a war neither side could win. The Allies and the Central powers were locked in trench warfare

DOUGHBOYS AND OTHER NICKNAMES

How American soldiers came to be called doughboys is unclear. The name might have come from the fact that even low-ranking soldiers in the AEF were paid more than European soldiers, so the Americans always had money—or "dough"—in their pockets. Another source for the name might have been the US Cavalry's service in Mexico. Members of the cavalry called foot soldiers "dobies" after the adobe huts used in Mexico. The British and French used other nicknames for the US troops, most notably "Sammie," a reference to the patriotic figure Uncle Sam. But once journalists began using "doughboy," that nickname was the one that stuck.

The armies of Europe had been pummeling each other at battlefields such as the Somme for three years before fresh American troops joined the fight.

that was killing hundreds of thousands of men yet bringing the end of the conflict no closer. British and French troops were worn down after three years of fighting. US military leaders were shocked the British and French did not coordinate their military strategies. They soon realized they would need hundreds of thousands more men to fight in Europe if the Allies were going to win.

On the Western Front, the Allied forces and the German troops each had tried to break through the other's front lines multiple times before the United States entered the war. These attempts to break through resulted in famous battles, including the First Battle of the Somme and the Battle of Verdun. Although US forces started arriving in France in the summer of 1917, they largely stayed in areas where there was not as much fighting in order to receive more training. Americans did not see much fighting until 1918. But once they reached the front lines, American soldiers helped to finally break the stalemate of World War I.

LIFE IN THE TRENCHES

The troops on the front lines had to worry about bullets, bombs, and poison gas attacks. Those were not their only worries, however. Enemy action aside, life on the front lines was miserable and dangerous. The soldiers, who lived in trenches dug into the earth, shared their space with bugs, vermin, and the dead bodies of their comrades. Bodies could be buried only when there was a break in fighting. When the soil shifted during battles, soldiers would sometimes encounter partially buried bodies.

A NEW KIND OF WAR

When the United States entered World War I, the US Army still saw the cavalry as its most important formation. The cavalry formation was based on officers mounted on horses with soldiers on foot charging the enemy. The formation had been in use for generations, and it had worked for the United States in its most recent clashes against the weak armies of Cuba, Mexico, and the Philippines. US military leaders were not yet aware of how different the combat in World War I had become, even though the war had been going on for three years. Horses were still used in World War I, but so were modern weapons, including poison gas, flamethrowers, and high-explosive shells. Other new technologies that made major impacts on the battlefield included aircraft, machine guns, submarines, and tanks.

The airplane was one of the key technologies that made World War I different from every war that came before.

SHELL SHOCK

In 1915, British physician C. S. Myers coined the term *shell shock* to describe the psychiatric problems he was seeing in soldiers coming back from the front lines. These problems included nightmares, sleep loss, and panic attacks. Sometimes psychiatric problems showed up as physical symptoms such as paralysis, the inability to speak, or uncontrollable shaking. There were many difficulties that could cause soldiers to suffer from shell shock. Some suffered from this disorder after being injured or due to the mental and physical stress of constant danger. Others developed shell shock because they were anxious about having to kill people. Doctors at that time started recognizing war could hurt a soldier's mind as much as his body. But they lacked experience and knowledge about how to treat mental disorders. Doctors tried hypnosis, psychotherapy, and even electric shocks. None proved very effective in treating the disorder.

They all increased how devastating and frightening war could be. The terror caused by artillery and other traumatizing weapons led to widespread cases of shell shock, a severe feeling of helplessness. Today, this is known as post-traumatic stress disorder. Advances were also made in medicine, but medical science struggled to keep up with the increasing lethality of modern warfare.

FIREPOWER IN THE AIR AND WATER

Airplanes are one of the best-known technologies to have had an effect in World War I. Invented only 11 years before the war began, by

STORIES FROM THE WAR

First Lt. George Brown Sheppard, an American army soldier who served in France, wrote a memoir in which he recollects the experience of a gas attack:

"At 11 o'clock a series of sharp detonations occurred in our vicinity. We rushed out of the dugout to observe causes and effects, while the explosions continued at regular intervals directly in front of us about where our grenade throwers were posted. . . . I sent the sergeant to see if the men were all right and he found them unhurt but excited. In the meantime the noise awoke the squad of trench mortar men who had been asleep in their shack and they came stumbling headlong toward me, crying, 'Gas, gas, gas,' and adjusting their masks."[1]

1915 airplanes had been adapted into efficient airborne killing machines. The British possessed only a handful of aircraft in 1914, but by the war's end they flew 22,000.[2] The Germans had about the same number, and the French possessed even more. At first, armies used airplanes for simple reconnaissance missions, using the elevated viewpoint to get a bird's-eye view of the battlefield. Advances in photography during the war allowed military leaders to use aerial photographs to better plan their strategies.

Airplanes also became weapons. In the first air-to-air fights, pilots shot at each other with handguns or rifles. Improvements were quickly invented. The German airplane manufacturer Anthony Fokker developed a device that synchronized an airplane's propeller with a machine gun, which meant the machine gun could be

ZEPPELINS

Military officials in Europe and the United States started experimenting with airplanes in the early 1900s, but Germany decided to pursue a type of flying airship designed by Count Ferdinand von Zeppelin. These rigid airships filled with lighter-than-air gases, known as zeppelins, were essentially enormous balloons. Germany eventually adopted airplanes for military use. First, though, it sent zeppelins on bombing missions over Belgium and the United Kingdom, killing or wounding hundreds of civilians.

fired straight ahead while the propeller was spinning without hitting the blades. The Allies duplicated the technology. Soon the battles in the air were as ferocious as those on the ground, and news of the daring pilots made some airmen famous. Airplanes also took on an air-to-ground role, with pilots loading their airplanes with bombs to drop on the trenches below.

The submarine underwent a similar evolution during the war. At first, military leaders used submarines mostly for reconnaissance and patrolling waters. Then the Allies and the Germans began using them to attack

FLYING ACES

The battle successes of pilots during World War I were well known by people on the home front. Germany was the first country to publicize its combat pilots. Starting in January 1916, German leaders sought to boost morale by detailing and celebrating pilots' exploits. They publicly awarded medals to pilots, passed out photographs, and taught about pilots in schools. The Allies did not approve of this practice at first, believing it was inappropriate. But they soon started promoting their own pilots. The French publicized pilots who had shot down five or more planes. This was the start of the "ace" system. Skilled pilots from all warring nations were soon known as "aces." The publicity made some pilots famous, but the practice was criticized for glamorizing combat and encouraging inexperienced pilots to take risks so they could have their turn in the spotlight.

each other's navy. The Germans developed faster submarines equipped with stronger weapons, making them even more powerful and destructive. Germany also used submarines to attack civilian ships and commercial ships carrying supplies to the Allied nations.

HEAVY WEAPONS

Both sides used machine guns, relying on the weapons more and more as the war progressed. At the start of the war, each army issued two machine guns to each battalion of approximately 1,000 men. But by March 1918, each German division of nine battalions had 54 machine guns and 144 automatic rifles. Each French division had 72 machine guns and 216 automatic rifles. And each British division had 64 machine guns and 192 light machine guns.[3] Automatic rifles and light machine guns were typically carried by an individual soldier. Machine guns were larger and often required multiple soldiers or assistants to operate. The stalemate on the Western Front was caused in large part by the machine gun and barbed wire, both invented by Americans.

The widespread use of machine guns made attempts to cross no-man's-land virtually suicidal.

The invention of the tank made it possible to smash through obstacles on the front lines.

Tanks also became increasingly important during the course of the war. British Army officer Ernest Swinton came up with the idea of using an armored vehicle to break through enemy lines. He thought the vehicle could help end the stalemate on the Western Front. The United Kingdom developed tanks by putting caterpillar tracks on tractors so they could cross uneven terrain. The army installed machine guns on the tanks to give them offensive firepower. The British used tanks for the first time on September 15, 1916, but they did not work very well and many broke down. The British continued working on tanks and developed new models, including the Mark IV. A year later, on November 20, 1917, the

British used 400 Mark IV tanks to break through German lines at the Battle of Cambrai.[4]

The Americans and French also saw tanks as important new weapons. However, the Americans did not have enough time to build tanks of their own, so they used French and British tanks. Germany underestimated how important the tank would become for fighting battles in World War I. It failed to invest in a sizable number of the new weapons. By 1918, it possessed only ten tanks.[5] Though Germans found ways to destroy enemy tanks, including specialized bombs and guns, their lack of the new motorized weapons left them at a severe disadvantage.

HORSES AT WAR

Some of the fighting that happened during World War I relied on tactics developed during past eras. One of those tactics was the use of horses. Some horses carried officers and soldiers into battle as part of cavalry units, while others were workhorses that pulled and carried equipment. When the war began in August 1914, countries throughout Europe called up hundreds of thousands of horses. Britain readied 165,000 horses, the Austro-Hungarians readied 600,000, the Germans readied 715,000, and the Russians rounded up more than 1 million.[6] Like the soldiers with whom they worked, these animals were subjected to bombs, bullets, injuries, and death.

WAR AND SOCIETY

When the United States entered World War I, the country finally started to fully mobilize. One of its first tasks was building its army. The US Army was largely a reflection of American society at the time. The country was home to many recent immigrants, and so was the military. Approximately 18 percent of military recruits were born in other countries, and many did not even speak or write English fluently.[1] American Indians joined the military, too. However, the army was not inclusive for all. White foreign-born US residents could fight side by side with native-born white Americans, but black Americans were still segregated into separate units—a result of the racism that prevailed in the United States at the time. Black leaders pushed army leaders to at least train blacks as officers. Secretary of War Newton D. Baker reluctantly agreed,

A segregated unit with white officers marches down Fifth Avenue in New York City.

AFRICAN-AMERICAN SOLDIERS

Racism was very much a part of the AEF, and there were different standards for blacks and whites at every level of service during World War I. Blacks and whites could not serve in the same unit. And black soldiers, after they finally won the right to train as officers, were not allowed to lead white soldiers. Some black soldiers, however, were assigned to French divisions that did not segregate their troops by race. The war effort united African Americans in an effort to gain civil rights at home after fighting for their country abroad.

creating a new camp to train them. But he would only assign black officers to black units.

WOMEN AT WAR

Women also faced many obstacles during the World War I era. They were not allowed to serve in the military alongside men, and many did not have jobs at all. Middle-class and upper-class women rarely worked, and women who did work could take only certain jobs, such as a textile factory employee or a secretary. Most women did not go to college or get professional training. In most of the country, women were not even allowed to vote. However, many American women found ways to serve their country and the Allied forces. Starting in 1914, almost 10,000 of them traveled to Europe to help the Allied nations.[2] They volunteered largely as nurses or cooks. After the United States entered the war, more than 16,000 American women served overseas, either as part of the AEF or as volunteers with organizations supporting the military.[3] Women even worked near the front lines as ambulance drivers, clerks, cooks, and telephone operators. The US Army refused to enlist women, but the navy and marines allowed it. Women recruits held mostly secretarial jobs, but they still earned military ranks. They were not allowed to serve in combat roles.

At the same time, women on the home front entered the civilian workforce in greater numbers. Companies lost their male workers to the military, so they hired women for positions they never would have had before in munitions factories. Women also expanded their

CODE TALKERS

Although the US military did not treat its black soldiers as equal to its white soldiers, the treatment of American Indians was in some cases better. A few American Indians were given roles critical to the war effort. The military gave some of them the task of relaying important messages. The military used American Indians, many from the Choctaw tribe, as telephone operators and had them speak in their own native language. They could transmit information without fear of Germans intercepting it because the Germans were not able to translate their language. Still, the Choctaws used code words within their language to further confuse any Germans who might have intercepted their messages. For example, they used the words "three grains of corn" for "3rd Battalion."[4]

Women seeking the right to vote associated their struggle with female contributions to the war effort.

roles in positions some held before the war, such as office staff. In part because of women's impressive contributions to the war effort, President Wilson lent his support to the movement to give them the right to vote. The movement succeeded in 1920 with the passage of the Nineteenth Amendment to the US Constitution.

ATTACKING WAR CRITICS AND FOREIGNERS

Not all men and women wanted to help the war effort. Many opposed the war. Some individuals were pacifists who opposed war altogether. Others did not want the United States to be involved in a foreign war. People's reasons for opposing the war differed, but all faced an American society that did not want to hear antiwar comments. A few of the people who opposed the war were attacked or killed. Even individuals who were only suspected of being sympathetic to Germany and its allies were attacked. On the other hand, there were

PACIFISTS BID FOR PEACE

The peace movement grew significantly during the first decade of the 1900s. Pacifists believed war was an outdated way to settle disagreements, and they formed peace groups to promote their ideas. One leader of the peace movement was Andrew Carnegie, who became rich making steel and later gave millions of dollars to establish the Carnegie Endowment for International Peace. Another leader was Jane Addams, a social worker and founder of the Women's International League for Peace and Freedom. Also active was Henry Ford, the founder of the automotive company that still carries his name. On December 4, 1915, he led a group of pacifists as they departed on a ship from Hoboken, New Jersey, setting sail for Europe, where they hoped to negotiate a peace agreement between the warring countries. The effort failed.

Americans who came together to defend the right of people to express their opinions and to help stop the attacks on those who opposed the war.

The war era was not easy for people from other countries. The United States locked up many foreigners because they came from Germany and other enemy countries. Others were German citizens living in the United States. President Wilson used parts of old laws known as the Alien and Sedition Acts of 1798 to make special rules against German men living in the United States. He called them "enemy aliens" and warned them that if they did anything that seemed suspicious they could be arrested.[5] The Espionage Act of 1917 and its amendments, commonly known as the Sedition Act of 1918, made it illegal to criticize the government in time of war. Despite heavy criticism by free speech advocates, the law passed easily.

THE WAR ECONOMY

Before the war, in 1916, the US government had established a Council of National Defense. Its mission was to coordinate the production of farms and factories, determine the most efficient ways to transport goods and people, and keep the public informed and passionate about the war. Its work was eventually delegated to the state level; every state created its own council. The councils helped raise money for the war effort through war bond drives. These bonds, known as Liberty Bonds, were essentially loans to the government. Citizens could purchase a bond, which would accumulate interest. After the war, it could be exchanged for money again. The councils also forced people to sign loyalty oaths, shamed those who avoided the draft, and boycotted newspapers they did not consider sufficiently patriotic.

The US government also set policies to make sure workers in jobs particularly important to the war effort, such as shipyard workers and loggers, did not disrupt work by going on strike.

SABOTAGE ON US SOIL

The battles of World War I occurred mostly in Europe, with some battles in Africa, the Mediterranean, the Middle East, and the Pacific. But the United States itself, separated from the conflict by two enormous oceans, was safe from full-scale attacks. Still, there were dozens of suspicious accidents or proven acts of sabotage on US soil during the war. In one case, a German-born US resident tried to blow up a railway bridge in Maine linking the United States with Canada. In another case, an explosion on July 30, 1916, at the Lehigh Valley Railroad's Black Tom Island ship-loading terminal in New Jersey killed three people and destroyed $20 million worth of munitions.[6] German agents were suspected of placing the bombs that destroyed the terminal.

Will you help the Women of France?

SAVE WHEAT

They are struggling against starvation and trying to feed not only themselves and children but their husbands and sons who are fighting in the trenches.
UNITED STATES FOOD ADMINISTRATION

The US government encouraged citizens to save food for the war effort.

At the time, labor movements were active in the United States, and strikes were frequently used to improve working conditions and pay. To help keep workers happy, the government encouraged companies to pay high wages. Government officials also drafted or threatened to draft workers who tried to go on strike.

The war affected companies in another way, too. Many companies had more work to do because of the war. The government hired companies to make all the items it needed to fight the war and support the troops. Companies supplied everything from lumber for building training camps to food for feeding the troops to uniforms for equipping soldiers. But many companies found themselves without enough workers. Many of the men working for them joined the military, and the immigrants who came to the United States to work in factories in the early 1900s stopped coming to the country once the war started. Many companies started hiring more black workers. These workers moved from southern rural states, where they faced more racism and fewer job opportunities, to the northern cities where most factories were located. During the war years, more than 300,000 blacks moved from the South to northern cities such as Chicago, Illinois, and Detroit, Michigan.[7] This movement became known as the Great Migration. It reshaped demographics not just in northern cities, but also in the areas that migrants left behind.

THE FINAL PUSH

The world entered 1918 with a bleak outlook. The war between the Allies and the Central powers continued, and the two sides remained in a stalemate. Soldiers were still suffering from all the dangers of the front lines. Americans at home lived with reduced freedoms and worry for their loved ones away at war. Some of the warring nations were running out of men to send to war. Austria-Hungary, for example, was so short of men that in 1917 it started drafting males as young as 17 years old.

Russian troops had departed the Eastern Front in late 1917 after Communists overthrew the Russian government. In the Treaty of Brest-Litovsk, signed on March 3, 1918, Russia officially exited World War I and gave up control of its Eastern European lands, including Estonia, Latvia, Lithuania, Poland, and Ukraine. Governments controlled by Germany would soon rule these countries. As a result of peace on the Eastern Front,

The signing of the Treaty of Brest-Litovsk removed Russia from the war, leaving the remaining Allies to contend with the full might of the German war machine.

RUSSIAN REVOLUTION

The Russian Revolution was one of the most important turning points in World War I. By 1917, Russian troops had suffered through several years of horrible fighting and significant losses along the Eastern Front. Russians at home suffered nearly as badly. They did not have enough food or fuel. Their frustrations were turning violent, and they started rioting, looting, and talking about overthrowing their monarch, Nicholas II. As the country descended into civil war and Communists took control of the government, Nicholas II and his family were executed in July 1918.

Germany was able to move most of its troops from the Eastern Front to the fighting on the Western Front.

The loss of Russia left the United Kingdom, France, and the United States facing Germany without one of their biggest allies. But Germany also lost allies toward the war's end. Austria-Hungary, Bulgaria, and Turkey were worn down by 1918 and unable to aid Germany in its fight on the Western Front. Meanwhile, a terrible strain of influenza was circulating the world. The number of soldiers and civilians sick or dead from the disease—estimated at up to 50 million—further impaired war efforts in all countries.[1]

At the start of 1918, the Western Front zigzagged hundreds of miles from the Belgian coast through France to Switzerland.

In terms of equipment, the Allies were better armed: they had 18,500 artillery pieces, 4,500 airplanes, and approximately 800 tanks. Germany, on the other hand, had 14,000 artillery pieces, 3,670 airplanes, and only a handful of tanks.[2] But Germany appeared to have a stronger position when it came to the number of soldiers. The Germans had 170 divisions against 54 British and 93 French divisions. Divisions usually consist of between 12,000 and 20,000 soldiers. There were 180,000 American soldiers in France at the time, with only 85,000 of them serving as part of combat forces.[3] The Germans showed their strength when they went on the offensive on March 21, 1918, breaking through the Allied front lines. The Allied losses were high. Between March 21 and May 2, more than 300,000 British and French troops were killed or wounded.[4]

THE SPANISH FLU

The final year of World War I saw one of the era's most destructive forces: a worldwide influenza epidemic. The exact source of the disease has not been determined, but historians have speculated it may have begun in Kansas. The so-called Spanish flu tended to hit young people the hardest. In fact, one in every three American soldiers that got the flu died from it. The spread of the flu started to slow in the fall, but in the end the disease killed more people than died in combat during World War I.

By 1918, both sides' trenches were elaborate and well fortified.

AMERICAN FORCES FLOOD INTO FRANCE

Approximately 1 million American soldiers arrived in France between April and July 1918.[5] The American forces had not engaged in many battles during most of their first year in France, but that soon changed. On April 26, 1918, the Germans launched a relatively small-scale raid on the village of Seicheprey, which was held by the US military. The Germans overran the American soldiers and captured Seicheprey. More than 650 Americans were dead or wounded.[6] It was the worst loss for the AEF up to that point in the war.

The United States then went on the offensive. On May 28, an American division attacked the Germans at a French village called Cantigny, capturing it from the defenders. In June, American forces attacked the Germans at Belleau Wood, capturing the small forest by the end of the month.

Still, the Germans were far from defeated. On July 15, they launched another major offensive, this time against French forces. But the French had learned in advance about the German plans, and they were prepared for the assault. Within a few days of the German attack, the French counterattacked. This battle, called the Second Battle of the Marne, was a turning point in the war. The Allies began to take the advantage, and Germany now had to focus on defending its own territory.

GERMANS REVOLT

German soldiers were not the only ones affected by the war. German civilians also felt the hardship of four years of fighting. Because the British Navy had blocked shipments going into Germany, Germans could not get enough food and supplies. The government rationed these items, limiting how much of them individuals could get. Some items were in such short supply that Germans had to improvise. Bread sometimes included sawdust and ground-up straw as filler. Clothes were made from paper. By the fall of 1918, Germans were fed up with the war. Workers refused to work. Some sailors mutinied. People were rioting in the streets. The German government wanted Emperor Wilhelm II to step down from the throne to end the war. At first he refused to quit, but he decided to abdicate when he saw people in the street rejoicing after a false newspaper report said he was no longer king.

BREAKING THE STALEMATE

The Allies attacked German forces again on August 8 at Amiens, France. The Allies managed to keep the plans for the attack a secret, so the Germans were surprised by the assault. The Allies fielded divisions from France, Canada, the United Kingdom, Australia, and the United States. And they carefully coordinated their attack, using planes, tanks, artillery, and troops together. The attack did not end the war, but the German military called it "the greatest defeat which the German Army had suffered since the beginning of the war."[7]

At this point, the presence of the American troops was being felt. More than 1 million US troops were already in Europe and 300,000 more were arriving each month by the fall of 1918.[8] AEF forces were engaged in more and more battles. They were key to winning the Battle of Belleau Wood as well as clashes at Meuse-Argonne and Saint Mihiel.

The Allies continued pushing Germany out of France and the Flanders region of Belgium in a series of decisive battles. Many German troops looted homes, destroyed buildings, poisoned water wells, and cut down fruit trees as they retreated. The towns and cities on the front lines of World War I had mostly been destroyed, but Allies also found some areas previously occupied by the Germans were still relatively untouched. The Belgian town of Menin, for example, had tiny brick houses and shops that were not damaged by the war.

By the end of September, some German military officers realized they were losing the war after four years of stalemate. German leaders in Berlin sent notes to President Wilson asking for a truce to end the fighting. Germany did not agree to some of President Wilson's terms, including his demand for the German emperor to step down. So Germany continued fighting.

French military leader and Allied Supreme Commander Ferdinand Foch assigned US forces to a part of the front lines known as the Saint Mihiel salient in France. The term *salient* was used often in World War I to describe the territory held by one side that jutted out into the territory held by the other side. German-held territory around the town of Saint Mihiel extended into Allied lines. US General John Pershing, who commanded the American troops, saw the opportunity for a decisive victory over the Germans at Saint Mihiel. He thought a victory there would put the Allies in a position to capture more land from the Germans in future battles.

Pershing had under his command 1,481 aircraft, mostly French made and flown by French pilots.[9] He also had 3,000 pieces of heavy artillery, the largest concentration of artillery to that date.[10]

By the summer of 1918 the strategic importance of a German defeat at Saint Mihiel seemed relatively insignificant; Allied leaders believed it was more important to capture other areas held by the Germans. But at the same time, they believed a victory at Saint Mihiel would boost morale. The battle was

US forces used machine guns to push German forces out of the Saint Mihiel salient.

seen as an opportunity to prepare US soldiers for the more critical battles ahead.

The Americans launched the offensive at 1:00 a.m. on September 12, 1918, and progressed quickly. By the evening of the next day, Pershing's forces had pushed the Germans back from the salient. The United States reported 7,000 soldiers killed or wounded in the two-day battle.[11] The skirmish demonstrated to the United States and its allies the nation's ability and willingness to fight.

WILSON'S FOURTEEN POINTS

When German leaders reached out to President Wilson in October 1918 to negotiate a peace treaty, they already knew much of what would be expected of them. President Wilson had outlined the terms for peace and the postwar world in a speech he gave to Congress on January 8, 1918. The terms were called the Fourteen Points. The key points Wilson wanted to include in the peace treaty included more open diplomacy to avoid secret pacts between countries and free sea travel for all countries. The plan also called for more open trade and commerce between countries and the creation of an association of nations to resolve international disputes.

Even as the leadership refused to give in, German civilians, workers, and soldiers were beginning to protest the war and the hardships it had brought. Kaiser Wilhelm II gave up his throne and left the country on November 10. Finally, Germany agreed to an armistice that started at 11:00 a.m. on November 11, 1918. World War I ended on the eleventh hour of the eleventh day of the eleventh month.

French civilians returning to their homes during the Allied advances often found only rubble where their houses once stood.

The Meuse-Argonne Offensive near the end of World War I came less than two weeks after the American assault on Saint Mihiel in September 1918. It was an enormous coordinated attack by all of the Allies across the entire Western Front. The battle lasted seven weeks and involved more than 1 million American soldiers.[12]

The Allies launched their attack on September 26, 1918. One of the chief goals of Allied Supreme Commander Ferdinand Foch was to hit the German railroads providing supplies. To achieve the objective, the United States assembled its largest military force to that date. They took the center, with French troops on their left and right. Supporting the infantry were 3,980 artillery guns along a 25-mile (40 km) front.[13]

The Germans countered the assault with their own artillery and poison gas. During the counterattack, the American "Lost Battalion" was trapped by Germans for five days in a ravine. Though it lost 360 of the 554 men who entered the ravine, the unit managed to defend itself long enough to allow other Allied forces to smash through the distracted German defenses.[14]

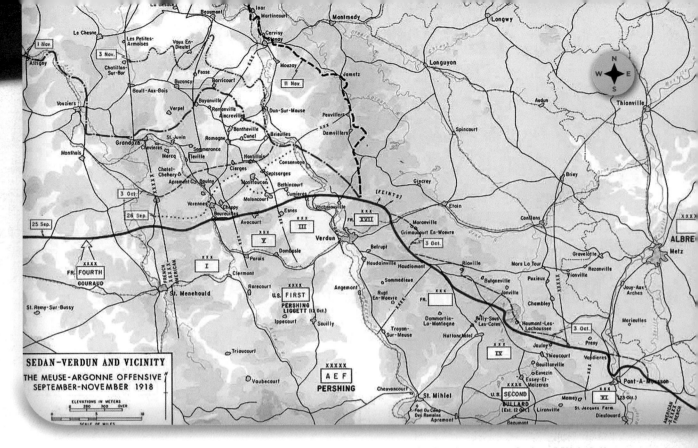

SEDAN-VERDUN AND VICINITY
THE MEUSE-ARGONNE OFFENSIVE
SEPTEMBER-NOVEMBER 1918

ELEVATIONS IN METERS
200 300 OVER

SCALE OF MILES

The Allied forces built upon their victory at Saint Mihiel (*lower center*), pushing the front west of Verdun (*solid red line*) steadily northward to the Armistice Line (*dotted blue line*).

Heavy fighting continued until the end of October. The Allies were victorious, but the victory came at a high cost. By the end, 98,000 members of the AEF were wounded and 26,000 were dead.[15]

8

THE ARMISTICE AND THE TREATY OF VERSAILLES

Journalists were some of the first Americans to hear about the end of World War I. They gathered in the middle of the night to hear a US State Department spokesman read a short statement: "The Armistice has been signed. It was signed at 5:00 a.m. Paris time and hostilities will cease at 11 o'clock this morning Paris time."[1] The news quickly spread. The *New York Times* had its early edition on the streets by 4:00 a.m. with the headline "ARMISTICE SIGNED, END OF THE WAR!"[2] Church bells, factory whistles, and firehouse sirens sounded, alerting people across the country the war was over.

American troops celebrated upon hearing the news about the armistice.

Although military officers anticipated the signing of the armistice, fighting continued in Europe right up until the eleventh hour. In fact, the commanders of nine of the 16 US divisions fighting on the Western Front on November 11, 1918, decided to keep fighting right up until the hour of the armistice. Some doughboys died that morning, just hours away from the war's end. One American soldier was shot and killed at 10:59 a.m.

The November 1918 armistice ended the war along the Western Front, but it did not bring instant peace to the world. There was civil war in Russia as well as in many of the countries surrounding it. There were many parts of Europe where the Allied troops could not enforce the rule of law, and these areas remained dangerous and violent places.

CASUALTY FIGURES

More than 70 million men were mobilized during World War I, and an estimated 9 million of them died. That means approximately one out of every eight died while fighting the war. Germany lost 2 million men, and the French lost 1.3 million.[3] Many millions more were injured. Some had arms or legs amputated. Others suffered from heart and lung diseases. A number of these injured men died of wounds after the war ended. Because a large number of the dead were young men, the generation of military age during World War I became known as the "Lost Generation."[4]

PEACE TREATIES

Although the armistice halted the fighting, it was not a permanent peace agreement. Leaders from the warring nations still had to work out a final treaty. To do that, they held the Paris Peace Conference in January 1919. Representatives from 37 countries attended the conference, including President Wilson. At first, the victorious nations formed the Council of Ten to work together. But the size of that group proved too large to take decisive action. So the leaders of the United Kingdom, France, Italy, and the United States came together in mid-March as the Council of Four to discuss the main issues that would go into the peace

POSTWAR LIFE

Even though fighting along the Western Front ended in November 1918, Britain continued its naval blockade of Germany through the winter of 1918–1919. That left people in Germany and much of Central Europe without needed food and supplies. Many areas, including Russia, faced years of famine following the war. Meanwhile, the war's end also created uncertainty for many people in Central and Eastern Europe because the Allies created new countries and boundaries during the peace process. The violent fights for power that followed in those areas caused more hardship for people and sometimes resulted in civil wars. Even citizens of victorious nations suffered from financial troubles as economies transitioned from war to peacetime.

treaty. However, leaders from the United Kingdom, France, and the United States ended up making the major decisions.

The Treaty of Versailles was signed on June 28, 1919, in the Versailles Palace, where the French royal family once lived. It was signed on the fifth anniversary of the assassination of Archduke Franz Ferdinand, the event that ignited World War I. The Treaty of Versailles officially ended the war between the Allies and Germany. Other nations, including Austria-Hungary, Bulgaria, and Turkey, agreed to sign separate peace treaties over the next two years. The United States refused to sign the Treaty of Versailles. It objected to a requirement to join a new international community known as the League of Nations, even though the league had been proposed by President Wilson in the first place. Instead, the United States signed a separate peace treaty with Germany. The treaty took effect November 11, 1921.

The Treaty of Versailles did more than just officially end the war. It tried to punish Germany. The treaty made Germany accept responsibility for the war, and it required Germany to return anything its forces stole from the countries it had

World leaders gathered in the Versailles Palace's Hall of Mirrors to sign the Treaty of Versailles.

occupied during the war. The United Kingdom and France wanted to reduce Germany's power in world affairs, so they looked to make the country weaker. Germany had to disarm most of its military, although it was allowed to keep a small army and navy strictly for defense. Germany had to give up some of its territory as well. The provinces of Alsace and Lorraine went back to France, while a large tract of land went to re-create the nation of Poland, whose lands had long been conquered by neighboring countries.

The treaty also required Germany to pay reparations to the Allies for the damage done. President Wilson wanted to limit how much

RESENTMENT ABOUT THE TREATY OF VERSAILLES

Germans resented the harsh terms set by the Treaty of Versailles. They criticized the postwar German government, called the Weimar Republic, for accepting these terms. One of the Germans frustrated with the government was a onetime aspiring artist named Adolf Hitler. He had served as a German solider during World War I. During the war, he was wounded by an exploding shell and briefly blinded by a poison gas attack. He read books that accused Jews of exploiting Germans and developed a belief in German racial superiority. Hitler wrote the book *Mein Kampf*, promoting his ideas of making Germany a world power by getting rid of its supposed enemies, including the Jews. He became a leader in the National Socialist German Worker's Party—also known as the Nazi Party.

Germany would have to pay. He wanted Germany to pay only for the damage it had done to civilians and their property. But British and French leaders wanted to make Germany pay much higher amounts, and they ensured this penalty was part of the treaty.

Several additional treaties were signed by the Allies and Germany's allies. These treaties sought to punish the countries for their role in World War I, requiring them also to pay reparations. The treaties redrew the map of Central Europe, creating the countries of Austria, Hungary, and Yugoslavia.

Many disagreed with the terms of the peace treaties,

THE TOMB OF THE UNKNOWN SOLDIER

Britain laid to rest the remains of an unknown soldier in Westminster Abbey in London in a grand ceremony on November 11, 1920, the second anniversary of the armistice. The country was the first to honor the many soldiers who had died during the war who were never identified. In 1921, the US Congress passed legislation to create the same tradition in the United States. Military leaders selected the body of one unknown American soldier taken from a battlefield in France. On November 10, 1921, the casket, draped in a US flag, lay in the rotunda of the US Capitol in Washington, DC. Thousands of people passed before the casket to honor the soldier's sacrifice. The next day, a military escort took the casket to nearby Arlington National Cemetery, where the body was laid to rest in what is now called the Tomb of the Unknown Soldier.

seeing them as too harsh in some ways yet too weak in other ways. The French military leader Ferdinand Foch was one of the people who believed the treaties were inadequate and would not bring a lasting peace to Europe. He said: "This is not peace; it is an armistice for 20 years."[5] He was right. Though World War I had been called "the war to end all wars," Europe would be at war again by 1939.[6]

People across the globe celebrated the end of the war, though a few suspected that the peace would ultimately prove temporary.

A NEW WORLD POWER

Nearly 3 million American men had been called to serve in the military, but the United States lost far fewer of its soldiers than the other nations that fought in World War I. Most came home quickly after the war ended. The United States discharged an average of 4,000 men every day from November 1918 through April 1919.[1] The government gave every discharged soldier $60 and a ticket home. It also allowed every soldier to keep his uniform along with one coat and a pair of shoes. Returning soldiers often displayed their helmets and gas masks. Meanwhile, filmmakers, writers, and painters displayed their reflections on World War I in a flurry of art during and following the war.

US soldiers returned from war-torn Europe to a nation that had emerged from the war relatively unscathed.

THE ARTISTS' VIEW OF WAR

Details, memories, and reflections about World War I appeared in a wide range of art both during and after the war. These pieces provided insight into what really happened on the battlefields and how people felt about the carnage. Some of the most important and memorable pieces of literature about the war include the *The Wasteland*, written in English by T. S. Eliot and published in 1922, *All Quiet on the Western Front*, written in German by Erich Remarque and published in 1929, and *A Farewell to Arms* by American writer Ernest Hemingway, also published in 1929.

Painters and graphic artists similarly created memorable depictions, such as *We Are Making a New World*, a stark painting of a ravaged landscape by British artist Paul Nash. Likewise, filmmakers sought to convey their interpretations in movies such as 1921's *The Four Horsemen of the Apocalypse*. One of the most enduring works is the poem *In Flanders Fields*, written by a Canadian physician, Major John McCrae, after a friend was killed in battle.

WILSON'S LEAGUE OF NATIONS

President Wilson went to Paris not just to negotiate a treaty but also to establish a new world order. He wanted a world where countries worked together to create stability and prosperity. As one of his Fourteen Points, Wilson proposed the creation of a League of Nations to help countries work collectively on the issues that affected all of them. He believed such an association of nations could work toward reducing the number of weapons in the world, ensure freedom around the globe, and promote commerce and international law everywhere. Although

Wilson disagreed with many parts of the Treaty of Versailles, particularly the parts that harshly punished Germany, he insisted the treaty establish the League of Nations. The League of Nations would be led by an executive council that included the Allied nations, and other countries would have voting power. Countries belonging to the League of Nations would agree to settle disputes through the league. Wilson thought the League of Nations could prevent future wars.

The majority of Americans supported the idea of the League of Nations, but they also disliked parts of it. Different groups found fault with different parts. A group of prominent women did not like that women had been excluded from the peace conference. They formed the International Congress of Women in 1919 and picked Jane Addams, an American voting rights leader, as its president. This group thought the treaty punished Germany too much, and it wanted all countries to disarm. Some black Americans did not like the fact that Africans in former German colonies in Africa were not part of the peace process even though the treaty determined the future of those colonies. Other Americans wanted to exclude the United States from parts of the League of Nations rules they thought went against American policies. Some opposed the league because they were isolationists; they believed the

THIS
LEAGUE OF NATIONS
BRIDGE
WAS DESIGNED BY
THE PRESIDENT OF THE
U·S·A·

BELGIUM FRANCE

ENGLAND·ITALY

KEYSTONE
USA

Political cartoonists and other commentators argued that without the membership of the United States, the League of Nations would be doomed to fail.

United States should remain isolated from world affairs. Some fought against the organization because they wanted the United States to be a strong, independent country making its own decisions. In the end, though the league was established, the US Congress voted against membership in it. Most other major nations, including the United Kingdom and France, joined it, but the league never lived up to Wilson's vision.

POSTWAR LIFE

Back in the United States, people were trying to adjust to life after the war, but it was not easy. Many people had been able to find work at good pay with good working conditions during World War I. But government orders for supplies stopped after the war ended, so companies did not need as many workers. They did not see the need to provide the same good wages or conditions, either. More than 4 million workers went on strike in 1919 to protest this situation.[2] Americans experienced race riots as tensions between black and white Americans continued. And people throughout

WOMEN GET THE RIGHT TO VOTE

President Wilson believed there were many reasons for the United States to fight in World War I, including his belief that his country's participation in the war could help spread democracy around the world. The National American Women Suffrage Association (NAWSA) supported the war and Wilson's promotion of democracy. NAWSA members encouraged women to perform patriotic work. But at the same time, they pushed for American women to be allowed to vote. They wanted to make sure President Wilson's push for democracy would include American women.

In 1918, Wilson endorsed a proposed amendment to the US Constitution that would give women the right to vote. Congress voted in favor of the amendment in 1919, and in 1920 three-quarters of the states voted in favor of it too. That was enough votes to add the amendment to the Constitution. As a result, the 1920 presidential election was the first one in which women throughout the United States could cast their votes.

The great cities of the United States survived the war completely intact, allowing the nation to quickly achieve dominance in the postwar world.

the United States became less tolerant of extreme political views, fearful about the possibility revolutions taking place in countries such as Russia could happen in the United States.

World War I ended a time called the Progressive Era, in which radical changes in society had been sought and accomplished. Despite the turmoil in the United States, the nation came through World War I much better off than the other countries that fought in the Great War. The United States did not suffer prolonged shortages of basic goods. It did not have battles fought on its land. It did not lose great amounts of livestock or farmland, as other countries had. It did not end up bankrupt economically or broken down emotionally. Instead, the United States emerged from World War I as a new power on the world stage. The nation became an economic power as other countries increasingly sought to buy the goods it produced. It also became a more important political ally for other nations. Even though some Americans sought to keep the country isolated, World War I proved the United States had an important role in foreign affairs. The Great War ushered the United States and its people into a century of dominance on the world stage.

AMERICAN SACRIFICES

There is no way to measure just how much US soldiers sacrificed to fight World War I, but some figures do help show how much Americans contributed. One of the most important statistics is the number of Americans who died: 53,500 men were killed in battle and 63,000 soldiers died from other causes, such as the flu. Another 204,000 men were wounded, and many of them lived with disabilities as a result of their wounds.[3]

JUNE 28, 1914

Assassins kill Archduke Franz Ferdinand, heir to the Austro-Hungarian Empire, sparking the beginning of World War I.

AUGUST 1914

The major European powers declare war on each other.

APRIL 22, 1915

In the Second Battle of Ypres, German forces use poison gas effectively for the first time.

MAY 7, 1915

A German submarine sinks the *Lusitania*, a British ship with Americans on board.

FEBRUARY 1917

The United Kingdom informs the United States about the intercepted Zimmerman telegram sent from Germany to Mexico.

APRIL 6, 1917

The United States declares war on Germany.

DECEMBER 1917

Russia exits the war, freeing up German forces to reinforce the Western Front.

JUNE 1918

US soldiers and Marines fight the Battle of Belleau Wood, one of the earliest US engagements of the war.

AUGUST 8, 1918

The AEF and the Allies launch a major attack on German forces at Amiens, France.

SEPTEMBER 26, 1918

The AEF and the Allies begin one of the last campaigns of the war, the Meuse-Argonne Offensive.

NOVEMBER 11, 1918

The Allies sign the armistice with Germany, ending the conflict.

JUNE 28, 1919

The Treaty of Versailles is signed, finalizing the details of the postwar world.

NOVEMBER 11, 1921

A separate peace treaty between the United States and Germany takes effect.

WORLD WAR I BATTLES, 1914–1918

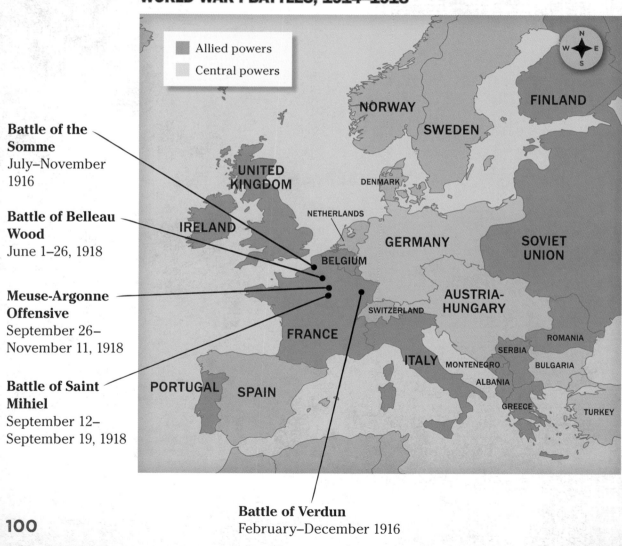

Allied powers
Central powers

Battle of the Somme
July–November 1916

Battle of Belleau Wood
June 1–26, 1918

Meuse-Argonne Offensive
September 26–November 11, 1918

Battle of Saint Mihiel
September 12–September 19, 1918

Battle of Verdun
February–December 1916

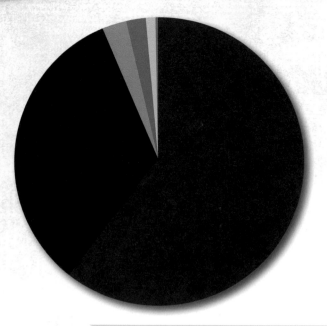

CASUALTIES

Total American Casualties: 320,518

- Army deaths: 106,378
- Navy deaths: 7,287
- Marines deaths: 2,851
- Army wounded: 193,663
- Navy wounded: 819
- Marines wounded: 9,520

KEY PLAYERS

US President Woodrow Wilson kept the United States out of World War I in the conflict's early years before seeking an official declaration of war in the spring of 1917.

US General John Pershing led the AEF in Europe.

Archduke Franz Ferdinand was assassinated in 1914, setting off a chain of events that led to the outbreak of World War I.

Emperor Wilhelm II led Germany during World War I, serving until public outcry forced him to step down and end the war.

artillery
Large weapons used to fire long-range explosives.

civilian
A person who is not a member of the military.

demoralized
Having lost courage, spirit, and discipline.

disarm
To remove weapons from.

lethal
Something that can cause death.

loot
To steal.

mobilize
To assemble and organize.

mutiny
To revolt or rebel against commanding officers.

reparations

Payments made to right a past wrong.

stalemate

A conflict in which neither side can win or move forward.

suffrage

The right to vote in elections.

vermin

Small animals that often carry disease.

SELECTED BIBLIOGRAPHY

Eisenhower, John S. D. *Yanks: The Epic Story of the American Army in World War I.* New York: Simon, 2001. Print.

Mead, Gary. *The Doughboys: America and the First World War.* Woodstock, NY: Overlook, 2000. Print.

Persico, Joseph E. *Eleventh Month Eleventh Day Eleventh Hour: Armistice Day, 1918, World War I and Its Violent Climax.* New York: Random, 2004. Print.

FURTHER READINGS

Adams, Simon. *World War I (DK Eyewitness Books).* New York: DK, 2007. Print.

Batten, Jack. *The War to End All Wars: The Story of World War I.* Plattsburgh, NY: Tundra, 2009. Print.

WEB SITES

To learn more about World War I, visit ABDO Publishing Company online at **www.abdopublishing.com**. Web sites about World War I are featured on our Book Links page. These links are routinely monitored and updated to provide the most current information available.

PLACES TO VISIT

The Museum of the Great War of the Pays de Meaux

Rue Lazare Ponticelli
Meaux, France 77100
+33 (0)1 60 32 14 18
http://www.museedelagrandeguerre.eu
The museum tells the history and the stories of World War I by using objects, including armaments and artillery as well as objects from daily life on the front.

The National World War I Museum

100 W. Twenty-Sixth Street
Kansas City, MO 64108
816-888-8100
http://www.theworldwar.org/s/110/new/index_community.aspx
The National World War I Museum has exhibits and programs to teach people about the experiences of the World War I era.

The Vintage Aero Flying Museum

7125 Parks Lane
Fort Lupton, CO 80621
303-668-8044
http://www.lafayettefoundation.org
This museum has one of the most significant and best-regarded collections of World War I memorabilia in the world.

CHAPTER 1. TRIAL BY FIRE

1. Gary Mead. *The Doughboys: America and the First World War.* Woodstock, NY: Overlook, 2000. Print. 229.

2. Ibid.

3. John S. D. Eisenhower. *Yanks: The Epic Story of the American Army in World War I.* New York: Simon, 2001. Print. 136.

4. Linda D. Kozaryn. "Marines' First Crucible: Belleau Wood." *American Forces Press Service.* US Department of Defense, 18 June 1998. Web. 28 Mar. 2013.

5. Ibid.

6. John S. D. Eisenhower. *Yanks: The Epic Story of the American Army in World War I.* New York: Simon, 2001. Print. 136–137.

7. Alan Axelrod. *Miracle at Belleau Wood: The Birth of the Modern US Marine Corps.* Guilford, CT: Lyons, 2007. Print. 8–19.

8. Ibid. 228.

9. Ibid. 179.

10. Linda D. Kozaryn. "Marines' First Crucible: Belleau Wood." *American Forces Press Service.* US Department of Defense, 18 June 1998. Web. 28 Mar. 2013.

11. Ibid.

12. John S. D. Eisenhower. *Yanks: The Epic Story of the American Army in World War I.* New York: Simon, 2001. Print. 148.

13. "USS Belleau Wood." *Dictionary of American Naval Fighting Ships.* Department of the Navy, 2007. Web. 28 Mar. 2013.

CHAPTER 2. A SHOOTING IN SARAJEVO

1. John Keegan. *The First World War.* New York: Knopf, 1999. Print. 10.

2. G. J. Meyer. *World Undone: The Story of the Great War 1914–1918.* New York: Random, 2006. Print. 113.

3. John Keegan. *The First World War.* New York: Knopf, 1999. Print. 198.

4. J. M. Winter. *The Experience of World War I.* New York: Oxford UP, 1988. Print. 143.

5. "Frequently Asked Questions about the Armenian Genocide." *Armenian National Institute.* Armenian National Institute, 2013. Web. 26 Mar. 2013.

CHAPTER 3. THE UNITED STATES ENTERS THE CARNAGE

1. Winston Groom. *A Storm in Flanders: The Ypres Salient, 1914–1918: Tragedy and Triumph on the Western Front*. New York: Atlantic Monthly Press, 2002. Print. 120.

2. Michael Beschloss and Hugh Sidey. "The Presidents of the United States of America." *The White House*. The White House, 2009. Web. 10 Jan. 2013

3. Maurice Matloff, ed. *World War I: A Concise Military History of "The War to End All Wars" and the Road to the War*. New York: David McKay, 1979. Print. 65.

4. Ibid. 35.

5. Ibid. 36–37.

6. Jay Winter and Blaine Baggett. *The Great War and the Shaping of the 20th Century*. New York: Penguin, 1996. Print. 118.

7. "Kapitänleutnant Walter Schwieger - Sinking of the RMS Lusitania, 1915." *Eyewitness*. National Archives, n.d. Web. 28 Mar. 2013.

8. Maurice Matloff, ed. *World War I: A Concise Military History of "The War to End All Wars" and the Road to the War*. New York: David McKay, 1979. Print. 66.

9. Woodrow Wilson. "President Woodrow Wilson's Address to Congress, April 2, 1917." *Library of Congress Internet Archive*. Library of Congress, n.d. Web. 28 Mar. 2013.

CHAPTER 4. THE UNITED STATES AT WAR

1. John S. D. Eisenhower. *Yanks: The Epic Story of the American Army in World War I*. New York: Simon, 2001. Print. 23.

2. Ibid. 25.

3. Neil M. Heyman. *World War I*. Westport, CT: Greenwood, 1997. Print. 72.

4. Gary Mead. *The Doughboys: America and the First World War*. Woodstock, NY: Overlook, 2000. Print. 47.

5. Ibid. 12.

6. Neil M. Heyman. *World War I*. Westport, CT: Greenwood, 1997. Print. 63.

7. Gary Mead. *The Doughboys: America and the First World War*. Woodstock, NY: Overlook, 2000. Print. 95.

CHAPTER 5. A NEW KIND OF WAR

1. George Brown Sheppard. "Memoir of George Brown Sheppard." *Veterans History Project*. Library of Congress, 26 Oct. 2011. Web. 28 Mar. 2013.

2. Winston Groom. *A Storm in Flanders: The Ypres Salient, 1914–1918: Tragedy and Triumph on the Western Front*. New York: Atlantic Monthly, 2002. Print. 83.

3. Hew Strachan. *The Oxford Illustrated History of the First World War*. Oxford, England: Oxford UP, 1998. Print. 145.

4. J. M. Winter. *The Experience of World War I*. New York: Oxford UP, 1988. Print. 100.

5. John Keegan. *The First World War*. New York: Knopf, 1999. Print. 393.

6. Ibid. 73.

CHAPTER 6. WAR AND SOCIETY

1. Neil M. Heyman. *Daily Life During World War I*. Westport, CT: Greenwood, 2002. Print. 23.

2. Ibid. 119–120.

3. Ibid. 120.

4. Phillip Allen. "Choctaw Indian Code Talkers of World War I." *Choctaw Code Talkers Association*. Choctaw Code Talkers Association, 2010. Web. 28 Mar. 2013.

5. Christopher Capozzola. *Uncle Sam Wants You: World War I and the Making of the Modern American Citizen*. New York: Oxford UP, 2008. 178–179.

6. Gary Mead. *The Doughboys: America and the First World War*. Woodstock, NY: Overlook, 2000. Print. 24.

7. Neil M. Heyman. *Daily Life During World War I*. Westport, CT: Greenwood, 2002. Print. 160.

CHAPTER 7. THE FINAL PUSH

1. Joseph E. Persico. *Eleventh Month Eleventh Day Eleventh Hour: Armistice Day, 1918, World War I and Its Violent Climax*. New York: Random, 2004. Print. 303–305.

2. Gary Mead. *The Doughboys: America and the First World War*. Woodstock, NY: Overlook, 2000. Print. 223.

3. Ibid. 208.

4. Ibid. 213.

5. Ibid. 222.

6. Ibid. 225–226.

7. Hew Strachan. *The Oxford Illustrated History of the First World War.* Oxford, England: Oxford UP, 1998. Print. 282–283.

8. Winston Groom. *A Storm in Flanders: The Ypres Salient, 1914–1918: Tragedy and Triumph on the Western Front.* New York: Atlantic Monthly, 2002. Print. 246.

9. John S. D. Eisenhower. *Yanks: The Epic Story of the American Army in World War I.* New York: Simon, 2001. Print. 188.

10. Ibid. 193.

11. Ibid. 194–197.

12. Jay Winter and Blaine Baggett. *The Great War and the Shaping of the 20th Century.* New York: Penguin, 1996. Print. 303.

13. Joseph E. Persico. *Eleventh Month Eleventh Day Eleventh Hour: Armistice Day, 1918, World War I and Its Violent Climax.* New York: Random, 2004. Print. 284.

14. Ibid. 294.

15. Ibid. 296–297.

CHAPTER 8. THE ARMISTICE AND THE TREATY OF VERSAILLES

1. Joseph E. Persico. *Eleventh Month Eleventh Day Eleventh Hour: Armistice Day, 1918, World War I and Its Violent Climax.* New York: Random, 2004. Print. 337.

2. Ibid. 337.

3. J. M. Winter. *The Experience of World War I.* New York: Oxford UP, 1988. Print. 206.

4. Ibid. 207.

5. Hew Strachan. *The Oxford Illustrated History of the First World War.* Oxford, England: Oxford UP, 1998. Print. 303.

6. "The War to End All Wars." *World War I Remembered.* BBC, 10 Nov. 1998. Web. 28 Mar. 2013.

CHAPTER 9. A NEW WORLD POWER

1. Neil M. Heyman. *Daily Life During World War I.* Westport, CT: Greenwood, 2002. Print. 259.

2. John Whiteclay Chambers II. *The Tyranny of Change: America in the Progressive Era, 1890–1920.* New Brunswick, NJ: Rutgers UP, 2000. Print. 269.

3. John S. D. Eisenhower. *Yanks: The Epic Story of the American Army in World War I.* New York: Simon, 2001. Print. 288.

ABOUT THE AUTHOR

Mary K. Pratt is a freelance journalist based in Massachusetts. She writes for a variety of publications, including newspapers, magazines, and trade journals. She has won several awards for feature and news writing.